ARYABHATTA

Aryabhatta was a famous mathematician and astronomer during the Gupta period. He is credited with the discovery of the 'decimal' system. For the first time in Indian history, he analysed astronomy and mathematics as two distinct fields of study. For a long time, he remained neglected. He was in the news and became a subject of discussion in 1975 when the Indian scientists sent a satellite into the space called 'Aryabhatta' after the name of Aryabhatta—the mathematician and astronomer.

It is believed that Aryabhatta was born in Ashmaka in modern Kerala in AD 476. Nothing more is known about his parents.

According to a scholar named S. Pillai, Aryabhatta was married and even had a son named Devrajan, who was also a great scholar of astrology.

It is believed that Aryabhatta received education at

Kusumpur (modern Patna). Later, he shifted to Nalanda to acquire higher education. There, he studied Prakrit, Apabhramsha and Sanskrit languages apart from the Vedas, the Upanishads and the philosophical treatises.

Ever since his childhood, Aryabhatta had been fond of novelty and innovation. It was his hobby to innovate something new out of broken toys. As he grew up, this tendency grew stronger.

He was against superstition and blind traditions and never accepted anything blindly. He used to examine and verify before accepting. Therefore, Aryabhatta never accepted the notion prevalent since Vedic times that the earth was stationary and the sun revolved around it. After several experiments, he had come to the conclusion that the sun is stationary and the earth revolves around it.

Aryabhatta has stated this conclusion as a principle in his work the Aryabhatiya. According to it, the earth moves a Kala during the period of one Pran (a measure of time).

In the 16th century, Copernicus, the famous western astronomer, propounded the same conclusion and principle.

It is a strange paradox that the discovery made by Copernicus had been hailed the world over, while the same principle, propounded by Aryabhatta 1,500 years ago, was severely criticised by Varahmihir, Brahmagupta, Lallacharya, who were his contemporary scholars. According to them, the discovery of Aryabhatta was against the traditional preachings of the Vedas and the Puranas.

Later, Aryabhatta was proved to be right. Therefore, Aryabhatta is, perhaps, the first scientist in the world to propound the Heliocentric Theory.

Aryabhatta initiated a new scientific tradition in opposition to superstition. His critics, too, had to accept his theory.

At an early age, he had acquired the knowledge of motion and position of the planets. In order to share his knowledge with the students, Aryabhatta took to teaching.

He was considered among the best teachers of his time. That is why he was honoured with the title of Kulapati (vice-chancellor) of a university.

It is believed that because of his merit and

scholarship, King Buddhagupta, the contemporary king of the Gupta dynasty, had made him Vice-Chancellor of Nalanda University. During the Gupta period, Nalanda University was the topmost centre of learning.

Later, some of the famous scholars such as Latdeva, Prabhakara, Lallacharya, etc. became the chief disciples of Aryabhatta.

Aryabhatta was recognised as a famous scientist and discoverer of his times. Therefore, the scholars of the past honoured him with several titles. Bhaskar-I (Bhaskar the First) honoured him with honorific titles such as 'Shreemabhatta', 'Prabho', 'Prabhu', etc.

Aryabhatta was the first scientist in the history of ancient Indian science to distinguish mathematics from astrology as an independent subject of study.

Aryabhatiya is, in fact, India's oldest astrological work completed by Aryabhatta at a young age of only 23 years in AD 499.

The completion of this original work was his great scientific achievement. Mathematical formulae have been included in it. This work demonstrates the keen intellect of Aryabhatta. It is divided into four

parts—Gitikapada, Ganitapada, Kalakriyapada and Golapada, in which there are 121 verses.

In his work Aryabhatiya, Aryabhatta has established a new thought that the earth is round and rotates on its axis, owing to which day and night takes place. At the same time, he has also maintained that the moon has no light of its own; rather it shines due to the reflected light of the sun. According to him, the earth and the other planets facing the sun get the light from the sun on one-half of the hemisphere, which faces the sun.

Aryabhatta propounded scientific reasons for the solar and lunar eclipses, which has nothing to do with planet 'Rahu' devouring the sun or the moon. Besides, he also made scientific explanations.

There are just 11 verses in the fourth chapter of Aryabhatiya wherein the subjects like the motion of the sun, the moon and the other planets, have been discussed. Besides, he has also explained the reasons for sunrise and sunset; shape of the North Pole; shape of the South Pole; definitions of astronomical mathematics; the method to find the root-number of the sun, the moon and other planets; appearance of only one-half of

the planetary bodies, etc.

In his work, Aryabhatta has propounded an amazing method of writing big numbers in a short way by means of 'Swar' and 'Vyanjan'—the letters of the 'Devanagari' script. According to it, the letter belonging to 'Ka' (in Devanagari) should be placed at even positions and those beginning with 'A' should be placed at odd positions. Similarly, 'Ang' and 'Ma' together become 'Ya'.

Unit, hundredth, ten thousandth, millionth, etc. at odd positions are known as square positions and tenth, thousandth, hundred thousandth at even positions are known as un-square positions because square roots of 1, 100, 100000 are complete numbers, but those of 10, 10000, 1000000 cannot be represented as whole numbers. He has used simple words to represent the big numbers. For example, he has used the word—'Ravyupta'—to represent 432,00,000.

In the third chapter, Aryabhatta has provided verses relating to the measurement of time. In it, he describes the units of time and angles, conjunction and disjunction of the planets, solar-lunar month, savan-nakshtra day, adhimas, kshaya-tithi, solar-year, divya-year,

classification of yugas, planetary motion and the time taken in revolution, measurement of the distance between planets and the mid-point of the earth, etc.

Aryabhatta was a highly proficient mathematician besides being an astrologer and astronomer. He has used a novel method to put in verses the astrologically useful numbers in the Aryabhatiya. He has used the 'Swar' and 'Vyanjan' letters of the 'Devanagari' script to depict the astronomical numbers. He has calculated the value of pi (p) as 3.1416 and found it as the closest value:

Radius from the value of pi = (3.1416)

The Aryabhatiya is a major work of astrology as well, wherein one finds several rigorous research-based theories by Aryabhatta. One finds a scientific analysis of time measurement. He said, "Time is eternal, unending and infinite." He divided it into several parts. He explained solar-day, lunar-day and constellation-day.

He observed heavenly bodies, planets and stars for years together before establishing the principles based on them. The measure of the distance of a yojan was found by him to be 9 miles. He established a new tradition of epicycle to determine planetary motion.

Therefore, some scholars gave him the title of the 'Father of Epicyclic Astronomy'.

According to Aryabhatta, planet earth consists of four elements—earth, water, fire and air. He also explained the gravitational force of the earth.

It is, therefore, ample clear that he was aware of the principle of gravitation much before Newton. Besides, Aryabhatta had established the Heliocentric theory, approximately 1000 years before Newton.

Aryabhatta proved that the height of atmosphere is approximately 109 miles from the surface of the earth, which is quite close to the current measurement. He was the first astronomer to propound and establish the new tradition of astronomical formulae.

Aryabhatta formulated and explained scientifically several principles as the length of the earth's shadow from the centre of the earth, etc. He established several formulae on planetary astronomy.

Like other Indian astronomers, Aryabhatta, too did his own research and gave different values for projection in his work. Scientists like Varahmihira and Brahmagupta followed the same tradition. The Aryabhatiya speaks of

one and the other three-dimensional figures and also discusses the method to construct them. The Arya-Siddhanta discusses about nine different types of 'Yantras' in detail. They are: 'Caya Yantra, Dhanur Yantra, Yashti Yantra, Chhakra Yantra, Chatra Yantra, Tope Yantra, Thatika Yantra, Kapal Yantra and Shanku Yantra.'

According to Professor D.E. Smith, Aryabhatta died at the age of 74 in the year AD 550.

□□□